PRAISE FOR *VANISHING* [...]

"With its complex imagistic shingling and sensitivity to a world accelerating its own erasure, *Vanishing Acts* serves as a countermeasure to the fear of such disappearance. These poems don't evaporate, they resonate. They 'rise in ecstatic waves' of the mythical, the marvelous, and the revelatory as Barker two-steps between tenderness and menace. Filtered through a fabulist lens, these cinematic compositions, with their salute to Francis Ponge, startle with extraordinary figurative language. Barker's poems are exquisitely bizarre documentations, both ethnographic and zoographic, lit with such intelligence and insight that I'm swayed to believe there's hope for us after all."
—Simone Muench, author of *Wolf Centos*

"*Vanishing Acts* is an archive of curiosities, an homage to the ardor of our exhausting, consuming, and beautiful preoccupations. Barker's imagination is as resourceful as it is original, repurposing whatever elsewheres it has at hand: the daddy longlegs, the elephants of Carthage, the Marquis de Sade reincarnated into a fly. The collection's title suggests the disappearance of a world we'll never know in the same way again, but this is also a book about what persists, what re-creates, and what refuses, beyond reason or the appearances of things, to ever really die."
—David Keplinger, author of *Another City*

"Barker's new book is a collection of darkly comic fabular prose poems for the 'nearly extinct.' He brings his sardonic humor, mythic sensibility, and linguistic inventiveness to these deadpan character-driven vignettes, apocalyptic beast fables, and dramatic monologues spoken by a range of quirky absurdists and grotesques. Although life in Barker's prose poems is marked by a sense of omnipresent menace, the abiding mood is one of wry appreciation of mystery and marvels, even at their most bizarre or calamitous."
—Anna Journey, author of *The Atheist Wore Goat Silk*

"*Vanishing Acts* is kaleidoscopic in its brilliance. These prose poems are gems in which wolves' 'fur coats will be like saints' beards soaked in wind,' grass sprouts from every step of the elk, and cottonmouths 'swim out of the hair of the drowned.' These poems are masterful and strange, depicting the twilight of human cruelty in a world on the cusp of rebirth. Inhabited by characters ranging from a strong man and Evel Knievel to a fish thief and monks, each of Barker's poems is cinematically adroit and lavishly steeped in a sacred gloom: a girl tells the police officer questioning her that the 'dog was clear like water, like a ghost trying to get in out of the rain'; soldiers killed in a civil war reenactment are forgotten and bereft of an opportunity for resurrection. Barker flourishes the approaching darkness with sparks and makes uncanny joys in his little, irresistible worlds."

—Alex Lemon, author of *Another Last Day*
and *Feverland: A Memoir in Shards*

VANISHING ACTS

CRAB ORCHARD SERIES IN POETRY
EDITOR'S SELECTION

VANISHING ACTS

POEMS BY BRIAN BARKER

Crab Orchard Review &
Southern Illinois University Press
Carbondale

Southern Illinois University Press
www.siupress.com

22 21 20 19   4 3 2 1

The Crab Orchard Series in Poetry is a joint publishing venture of
Southern Illinois University Press and *Crab Orchard Review*. This
series has been made possible by the generous support of the Office
of the President of Southern Illinois University and the Office of
the Vice Chancellor for Academic Affairs and Provost at Southern
Illinois University Carbondale.

Editor of the Crab Orchard Series in Poetry: Jon Tribble

Cover illustration: *Loot Bag*, a painting by Martin Wittfooth

Library of Congress Cataloging-in-Publication Data
Names: Barker, Brian, [date] author.
Title: Vanishing acts / Brian Barker.
Description: Carbondale : Southern Illinois University Press, 2019. |
Series: Crab Orchard series in poetry
Identifiers: LCCN 2018028871 | ISBN 9780809337279
(paperback) | ISBN 9780809337286 (ebook)
Subjects: | BISAC: POETRY / American / General.
Classification: LCC PS3602.A77547 A6 2019 | DDC 811/.6—dc23
LC record available at https://lccn.loc.gov/201802887

CONTENTS

One

Science Fair

One industrious young man has built a life-size replica of a Model T out of tin cans and Popsicle sticks. Slumped over the steering wheel is a legless mannequin dressed up like Ford himself: a mothballed wool suit, a bowtie stapled on just below the Adam's apple, a thin, brown wig leaking little curds of glue. From the abyss where the engine would be, a set of red jumper cables creeps out like an invasive vine, winding through the cafeteria, twisting around chairs and tables, snaking behind the high stainless steel counters, over the kitchen tile scalded with ammonia, and out a back door propped open so the mice can escape. A group of children and their teacher follow the cables out into the desert dusk, climbing a steep slope of scree to a plateau above the school. Here, a feverish Audubon in a bathrobe, his face pixelated with sweat, circles an eagle chained to a perch, jotting down measurements and notes. The cables disappear into a crude surgical incision in the center of the bird's chest. "John James Audubon, the father of modern ornithology," the teacher intones, wiping his spectacles with a dirty hankie. "*Aquila chrysaetos*—when Ford cranks the switch, it'll light up like a pinball machine!" The children nod, wide-eyed, open their notebooks, and poise their pencils. In one pocket of Audubon's robe, the heads of nestlings bob up and down like hot pistons. Their bald, pink cries keep filling in the blanks.

Uncle Z's Toupee

Uncle Z wears a toupee to hide the hole in the top of his head. Years ago, the secret police pistol-whipped him, down on all fours until the names rattled out, one at a time, like kidney stones into a metal bedpan. The hole they left never left him. When he lies down at night, the ghosts of names keep leaking from it, wafting like a chemical fog high into the atmosphere. On the bedside table, next to a glass of water and a little bottle of pills, bathed in the submarine glow of the alarm clock, the toupee rests, like the pelt of some extinct animal that whimpers softly in his dreams.

Strong Man

Vivian hovered over the stove heating a cup of milk for the Strong Man convalescing in our bathtub. We found him at the edge of the woods behind the house, facedown in the snow. A gang of children had scrawled obscenities all over his biceps and pecs, and a tiny row of blue blisters glistened on his upper lip like a mustache of radioactive lice. In those last hours of gravity, the night was a hush, except for the wooden spoon scraping the bottom of the iron pot. The cats sniffed the air beneath the bathroom door. When I peeked through the keyhole, I saw that he had switched off the lights. All I could make out were his shiny red tights rising in the dark, like a jellyfish billowing up from the bottom of the ocean.

Evel Knievel

He jumps mountain lions, man-eating sharks, a pit of rattlesnakes three feet deep. He jumps from skyscraper to skyscraper, over ten thousand hippies marching down Fifth Avenue. He jumps six Soviet battleships and a caravan of sheiks perched on camels. He jumps one hundred dead Hell's Angels stacked like flattened Impalas. He jumps the Great Wall of China at dawn and the Grand Canyon in moonlight. He jumps fifteen yellow school buses full of nuns and orphans. They wave pennants from the windows, pom-poms, streamers, and he jumps blindfolded, with no hands, spread-eagled while eating a bucket of fried chicken. He jumps and never comes down, floating on his motorcycle through the blue-black limbo of a coma. As his cape flaps in the stratosphere, he sweats through his hospital gown. His hair beneath the gauze skullcap still smells like gasoline. A nurse sponges his bruised testicles with one hand and hefts his gold belt buckle in the other. She lifts it to her cheek and dreams of the Aztecs, of the lost shield of Achilles. He's the last gladiator in the new Rome, and she feels the light from his broken bones crowd the room like jigsawed ghosts. Deep down in his darkness, he's squinting through a snow of confetti. He's sizing up the next ramp. He's revving his engine against destruction.

Elephant

We rode an elevator up the elephant's trunk to an observation deck between its eyes. There, we bought lemonade that sloshed from our cups each time the elephant took a step. Flies swarmed, big as buzzards. We fed a coin to the binoculars and could see poachers in the high grasses polishing their machetes. Still farther off, columns of smoke rose from the ruins of Carthage. We held hands as the sun set, knowing nothing would ever be the same.

The Land Agent

He's on the front porch wanting to buy your mountain. A band of sweat seeps through his hatband. When he mops his brow, his hankie comes away black. He has a long, bald prehensile tail that sends the cats skittering, and a bottomless briefcase full of maps that he unrolls with a flourish on the dining room table. He lords over them like a general, pointing, talking, pointing. There's coal beneath you that runs like a seam up the back of a stocking, or like the blue scar bisecting your grandmother's neck. "What about the dust?" you ask. "What about the explosions?" No problem! The top comes off clean, like a hat or a scalp. Later, in his rented room above the VFW, he mops the puddle of his face and draws the curtains, trying to keep the light out. (Lights from Chilhowie to Katmandu, forests of lights where forests used to be, halogens illuminating cathedrals of kudzu, empty mesas, parking lots where insomniac seagulls graze.) A sweet little gray-eyed ghost he met at the truck stop drops by. She's eighty-five pounds of air with a tar pit bubbling in her mouth. When she massages his purple bunions, the light shines right through her. His eyes roll back in his head and he mutters, "Honey, oh honey." He holds his rotund gut delicately, with two hands, as if he'd just devoured an enormous supper of dynamite.

In the Valley of Plenty

When you first arrive in the Valley of Plenty, you are given the Lord Jesus Christ as your Savior. You are given a small cup of water laced with gasoline to wash the soot from your teeth. You are given a mothballed quilt, a bar of homemade soap, a mousetrap but no cheese. In the Great Room after supper, you watch some old folks in rocking chairs try to nod off in front of the fire, but a fat cousin in footy pajamas tickles their earlobes with a bloody chicken feather. All night long a puzzle of gray snow lifts off the pines, and beneath your pillow, machines clang to the chuff of blood, to bones vibrating, a chorus of whistling piercing the smallest tunnels in the ear. At the edge of your sleep, the miners rise and walk off through the trees, their bright lamps bobbing like an orrery among the branches before they click them off. They turn up the collars of their coats and pass around a flask before climbing into a car propped on cinderblocks. They drive all night just to make it back home.

Vanishing Act

After the dust settled, the villagers were dumbstruck to find the mountain gone. Nothing remained but a wide ribbon of ash running westward like the cold contrail of a rocket. A blur of jays and starlings zigzagged overhead, shrieking, desperate for their nests. The women pulled their shawls tight around their shoulders and hugged themselves. There was something obscene about the horizon, and when the sun sank behind it, a few of the men, overcome with vertigo, held up their hats and vomited discreetly behind some bushes. The men left at dawn in a search party and never returned. Now, the widows live together in a rambling Victorian on the outskirts of town. They keep the curtains cinched shut and burn old books and furniture to stay warm, passing most afternoons by cleaning a small cache of firearms. Some nights, when the devil drums his painted nails against the picture window, they can be spotted chasing him back across the wasteland to his hole, running barefoot over the cold, powdery cinders where all sound perishes. Their long, white gowns trail behind them, flapping against the black arc of the universe, like so many moth-eaten sails.

Rural Electrification

The last catfish known to man drifts across the bottom of a lake, dozing in the shadow of a hydroelectric dam. She's as big as a Soviet submarine. The whiskers on one side of her face were sheared off by the propeller of a pleasure boat and never grew back. Though divers say she is docile and melancholy, her skin looks like a relief map of Mars and burns like dry ice to the touch. She trolls the streets of a town drowned years ago in the name of rural electrification, nibbling on chimneys, picket fences, shingles, gingham drapes, doilies, long strips of flowered wallpaper. On endless winter nights, when the loneliness is unbearable, she pokes her cudgel-like lip through the steeple window of the North Star Baptist Church and rings the old bell. Seconds later, the pealing jolts the surface. The gaggle of geriatric geese huddled beneath the bridge strain a few feet skyward into the darkness, then drop back to the half-frozen lake with a soft thud. The feathers on their gray necks stand straight up.

Symbiosis

In the GrowPods colonizing outer space, scientists are observing new and exciting forms of symbiosis. In one, the Abyssinian mud elk has exchanged its antlers for the cashew tree, which sprouts directly from the mighty beast's pate. Flourishing in the oxygen-rich environment, the branches produce nuts as fast as the golden flightless macaws can pluck and crack them. They drop the meat through the canopy to grateful one-armed sloths. These challenged arboreal browsers emerged from the jungles of Guyana at the end of the Million Year War, but no need to feel sorry for them. Our slow, smiling friends also get assistance from the translucent teardrop ant of the Lost Serengeti. This peculiar arthropod lives a solitary life in a small swath of fur just below the sloth's eye, grooming fleas from our happy amputee with its retractable, needle-like proboscis. Look closely and you can see its circulatory system, a tangle of freeways swimming with archaeans. These glowing little scavengers thrive on microscopic particles of plastic and traces of radioactive waste. Their diminutive kingdoms are full of hustle and bustle and throbbing with light. Scientists old enough to remember are reminded of the bygone cities of Earth, observed twinkling at night from the vantage of an aeroplane.

Two: Re-Creation Myths

Sea Anemones

They will be without language like the stone. Their neon tentacles will be like hippopotamuses dreaming of hair. They will shit where they eat and remind us that nature is a beautiful stomach. Desire will be refracted through them as if through a prism: any which way you turn them, they will be an open mouth. When the oceans rise, they will grow tongues and laugh at the darkness. They will climb toward heaven on their one foot. They will be puppets without eyes miming directions for the drowned.

Hippopotamuses

They will be the last behemoths of mud. Their heads will be like battered fedoras floating on the surface of a lake. Their torsos will be boulders percolating blood. When they haul themselves ashore, rivers will flow backwards, and cities, miles away, will blanch on the Richter. Their newborns will be like giant hardboiled eggs dredged in gunpowder. When they belch, fruit bats will glide from the caves of their stomachs and startle the moonlight. Their tiny ears will deceive. They will be deadly cartoons dancing a polka that disembowel man, woman, child.

Bats

They will crawl out of the ashes of cold barbecue pits. Their wings will be cut from the backs of chimney sweeps. They will hang from the antlers of an elk like a congress of drowsy trapeze artists. At dusk above houses, they will appear and disappear and appear, weaving a jagged cotillion through the trees. Their songs will travel before them like aneurysms on strings, shattering streetlights, car alarms, nerves. When winter comes too early, we will see their faces in our frostbitten fruit. Insomniac, they will be your alphabet at the window. Sleeper, they will be the jewelry of your death, tangled in silk pajamas, in a wet beehive of hair.

Elk

They will outrun the arrow and the bomb. They will lean against abandoned jalopies and sleep. Their great antlers will be antennas growing back to God, clipping power lines, crackling with sheets of radio static lifting toward the stars. When they graze at night, their heavy heads will be like hornets' nests nodding in the breeze. In the darkness, slugs will test the air from the tips of their tines. On the first day of spring, they will walk the crumbling highways into the cities of man. They will sharpen their horns on cornices and cement. Everywhere they step will sprout grass.

Slugs

They will be slow gelatinous bullets cutting forests into lace. Between wars they will climb down and suckle the tear ducts of the dead. When they copulate on cellar walls, their bodies will be like two poles of a battery frothing corrosion. After monsoons, they will be soft scholars scrawling iridescent notes on sidewalks and doors. They will gather at night to mob the plate glass window of a butcher shop. There, they will draft a brief treatise on murder above the severed head of a pig. The next morning, no one will notice it glistening in the sun.

Pigs

They will be jigsaw puzzles for the demonic. They will climb out of Hell on an escalator of their own shit. They will don furs and gold chains and chew on toothpicks. They will recline in scalding tubs to primp. When their doughy faces wink back from the blades of our knives, they will dream they are German porn stars vacationing on the Riviera. They will scramble into the sea like a pink rockslide of flesh. They will sweat lard and bleed into the tide. In slaughtered piles, they will peek through the keyhole of their neighbor's anus into a briny diorama where a lobster cuts up an octopus. They will grimace a placid smile. Even in death they will be condemned to die again.

Lobsters

In the depths of the sea, they will eat the sea and outgrow the world's largest pot. They will flash one claw for seizing Skee-Balls, beauty queens, crowbars, and French cigarettes. They will wield a second for crushing padlocks, testicles, school buses, and cops. At night, we will hear them on the roof and in the attic, clacking away like an escadrille of vulturous typewriters. We will find them clinging to curtains, curled beneath beds, wedged into air-conditioning ducts. Some of them will prefer to sit upright in armchairs, basking ceremoniously in the glow of reading lamps. When we tiptoe closer, they will grind the three teeth hidden in their stomachs. They will flex their speckled mandibles in a frantic gesture of loneliness and menace.

Turkey Vultures

They will reek of tire fires and scorched fur. Their heads, shrunken by boredom, will be like desiccated beets skewered by the sun. They will descend forever, singed dirigibles corkscrewing blue skies, dreaming of the tart tartare of armadillo, the rank sinewy tangle of wolf. In a roadside ditch, they will bow their mummified faces into the steaming bowl of a body and eat, and raise them again, their blood-red hoods lacquered redder by blood. At night, they will roost in a forest of metal trees, black pineapples ripening in the moonlight, downy cocoons waiting to be kicked open by an angel. They will be the first and last foreboding: spangles of soot blown away in a gust.

Three

Dream in Which We Eat the World

Creamed calf's brain and vodka in a farmhouse outside Krakow. Blood sausage and cold tripe salad. Borscht that sends a flush down your neck and collarbone. Our hostess, a crone who recites Mickiewicz, her enormous breasts shaking as she cackles and fans you with her apron. Her scent comes in black waves, licorice and berry blintzes, and we swoon on the hot winds of Santiago, where we eat smoked pig's cheek smothered in fire ant jam, rolled in plantain leaves, served in a box like expensive cigars. The peasants drag the dead dictator from the palace. They dump him in a field of thistles as bees buzz the soft skin behind his ears where he dabbed cologne each morning, cedar and orange peel lifting on the breeze, and we're drowsing off again, now a pair of spotted goats in love, nibbling his gold epaulettes, eating the cuffs off his silk shirt. But still we scarf down goat heart tartare in Barcelona, bone marrow on brown bread, giblets with a little salad of violet blossoms dressed in squid's ink that you lick from the plate. In San Miguel de Allende, our tongues savor tongue tacos with pickled onions bought from a child riding a blind burro. We eat them in silence in one bite, then drink cold beer under a jacaranda tree, toasting love and good luck. In Venice, octopus carpaccio with a dollop of urchin roe, drizzled with olive oil, sliding on a plate as big as a hubcap as the room tilts and green seawater rushes beneath the door, sloshing with claw and kelp, sardines shimmering in the candlelight. Our waiter brings more wine, galoshes, cracks his towel at an eel clinging to the tablecloth, then sweeps his hand down over the teeming dark waters: *Tonight, for you lovers, any desire you want.*

The Secrets of Eroticism

Evenings at the café, we smoked like French philosophers and graded freshman essays. In one, Hitler was a fierce anti-Semantic. In another, Texas employed the guillotine with impunity. You lifted a demitasse of cold, thick printer's ink to your lipsticked lips and stared at me knowingly. Beneath the table, our slippery sock feet grappled in secret. Meanwhile, the Marquis de Sade returned to the world as a fly. He lighted atop our bowl of sugar cubes, washing his face triumphantly.

Blizzard

Because he forgot his muffs, the snow blew sideways into the man's ear, showering down the long spiraling staircase into the Venetian ballroom tucked behind the cerebellum. The gold candelabras hissed like angry octopuses, but the dukes and duchesses smiled and waltzed on through ankle-deep drifts, gliding beneath their elegant wigs now wigged with snow. In the scullery, though, the servants could not contain their giddiness. A snowball fight erupted between maids and footmen. Squeals of laughter. Curses hurled over the clamor of falling pots and pans. When the man quickened his pace, covering his ear with a mitten, the windows darkened. A truce, a quick pairing off in cold closets and alcoves to suckle a bloody lip, to kiss an apple-shaped bruise throbbing just above a breast.

Experimental Mating Rituals for the Nearly Extinct

She was trying to mate the last Kanburi pit viper with the last rufous-headed hornbill, the idiotic kid! She locked them in her dollhouse and kept spraying her mother's White Shoulders down the chimney to "create the mood." The viper, suffering from post-traumatic stress, curled up in the den in front of the TV where a *Facts of Life* marathon looped endlessly. The hornbill was stricken with a rare type of mange and had already shed all its colorful plumage. A trembling boiled potato with a giant scarlet beak, it hid in my underwear drawer and refused to come out. I was a biologist with incurable insomnia, unshaven, apt to make late-night hoagies in nothing but my lab coat and bath slippers. I remember the girl's diabolical blue eye filling the night sky beyond the kitchen window, then the gleaming black point of a sharpened pencil trying to stab me as I ran from room to room. Now I've been hiding for days in an upstairs closet that smells of mothballs and mildewed mink. I've kept my ear pressed to the door, listening for the snake slithering up the stairs, or the bird squawking a mating call from beneath an avalanche of boxer briefs. *No signs of life*, I note daily on a chart I've scribbled on the wall, only the sound of canned laughter bubbling up through the floorboards.

Murder Ballad

Georg Wilhelm Steller married his sea cow in a simple ceremony on a Bering Island beach. Five scurvied crewmen bore witness. In lieu of rings, the couple exchanged garlands of kelp, which the blushing bride quickly devoured. That night, while she snored next to him, the naturalist wrote in his journal: *She is insatiable! Her skin is black and thick, gnarled like an ancient oak. Toothless, the space between her lips is packed with a dense array of thick bristles, the kissing of which I dare not describe. When her stunted flippers draw my head to her bosom, I feel the embrace of Eternity itself!* But rumors of infidelity spread quickly, until one evening, in a jealous rage, Steller buried a hatchet deep between her eyes. Afterward he recorded: *When confronted, she refused to confess. Like her species* in toto, *she proved mute and reticent, resigned to fate. Even when mortally wounded, she could barely manage a bellow. My beloved died like all her kind before her—quietly, heaving a deep sigh.*

Charon's Pawn Shop

Yes, that's *the* Trojan horse. Feel free to pop the hatch and peek inside. You can still smell the musk of the warriors who crouched in its belly. See the crawl space in the head where two spies contorted, gritting their teeth? In that old ice box in the back corner, you'll find the last breaths of illustrious killers sealed in jars—Jack the Ripper, Ted Bundy, Billy the Kid, some others. Hold them up to the light and they'll curl like blue smoke. Each is authenticated and can be packed in dry ice for your trip. In the glass case up front, you can browse a nice assortment of bric-a-brac—a lock of Sitting Bull's hair, a vial of Joan of Arc's ashes, the bullet that finished Hitler. This handkerchief staunched the gushing wound of Archduke Franz Ferdinand. Unfold it and you have a Rorschach of blood that makes for a unique parlor game. (I see a snake that swallowed a porcupine. What do you see, young lady?) If you're hunting a bargain, Cromwell's head is on sale, still grimacing after all these years, not a hair out of place. A good bar mitzvah present or, paired with Lincoln's stovepipe hat, a perfect gift for Father's Day or a groom-to-be.

Night Class at the School of Metaphysics

Forget the Chaldean oracles and the Minoan bull gods, the guest lecturer told us. It all comes down to simple arithmetic. Archimedes in the afterlife, hunched over an adding machine. He chews on the stub of a pencil, squints to crunch numbers by candlelight. He pulls the lever: *a forgotten Slovenian poet dies while drinking a glass of milk and gazing out the window at the moon.* The work makes Archimedes feverish. His feet are sunk in a bucket of ice, but blisters of salt still form on his eyelids. He pulls the lever: *one Ioseb Jughashvili is born in Gori, two adjoined toes on his left foot.* The machine unspools its skein of tape onto the floor. Waist-deep, it climbs the walls of his office in frothy waves. Once a week, he donates truckloads of the stuff to the local orphanage. The children use it to line their hamster cages, or to fashion fake beards for their play about Old Testament prophets.

Tubas

A military band squeezed inside a bomb shelter. Buttons bursting, plumes razing cobwebs draped from the ceiling. The flautists were crushed against a wall, wilting like lilies. The bored saxophonists primped in the bells of their horns. But the tubas loomed in the middle, blubbering back and forth like hung-over lumberjacks commiserating about a heat wave. The conductor tapped his baton, just wanting a moment of silence before the fire rained down. But the tubas, hammered from the bowels of walrus, kept bellowing, the red-faced men teetering beneath them. "Who was blowing whom full of bluster and menace?" we asked, when a team of oxen pulled their bodies from the rubble, still yoked to their Cyclopes, to those brass ampersands shining in the sun.

Blindfold

At the birthday party, when they blindfolded his grandson and spun him in front of the piñata, the old man dizzied in two worlds at once. For a month during the war, he had marched a prisoner out to the square and awaited orders to execute. Each day when he tied the blindfold, he watched the tendons in the prisoner's neck grow taut as the head strained to escape the body. Once, when the prisoner collapsed from exhaustion, the boy's grandfather lifted him back to his feet, saying, "Upsy-daisy," as the prisoner muttered, "Marie, Marie, Marie," and the children sucked helium from a balloon, clasped hands, turned in a ragged circle, singing "Ring around the Rosie." When the bombs began to fall, the soldiers scattered and left the prisoner standing in the dark. "Marie, Marie, Marie," he cried, the blindfold wet with tears, and the candy rained down like shrapnel into the grass.

Civil War

After the reenactment, someone forgot to wake the dead. Someone hosed down the cannons and horses. Someone rolled up the tents and folded the flags and sheathed the bayonets and polished the muskets. Someone packed up the maps and brass spyglasses and skillets and bugles and drums. Someone brought out the cooler of beer, and the lieutenants and generals gathered in the gravel parking lot and unbuttoned their long overcoats, laughing, leaning against a pickup truck. But sprawled in the meadow of high grass, in the thicket skirting the woods, the dead went on being dead. Bloodless and still, they were dreaming of perfection when the crowds dispersed and the woolly dusk began shagging the oaks. Hours passed, or days. A cell phone rang, but no one sat up to answer it. They gave over to mice nesting in their pockets, to deer nibbling at their eyelids, to snow scrimshawing their mustaches, to crows hopping triumphantly atop their chests. Eventually, though, their backs began to ache and they pined for their wives and kids. They grew nostalgic for the old days when the end was clear, when someone would stand in shadow at the edge of the field and shake a cowbell, and they would rise one by one, dazed, a bit stiff, brushing straw from each other's backs, passing around the battered canteens. A few would light cigarettes and mutter obscenities. "Who knew dying could be so damn hard?" some burly guy would always say, shaking his head, before the whole forgotten lot of them limped off into the night.

Four: Re-Creation Myths

Wolves

Their fur coats will be like saints' beards soaked in wind. Their eyes will be
bone buttons winking in the bramble. They will raid the barnyard, then trot
into town, leaving a loose crewel of bloody paw prints on the marble steps of
the opera house. In the orchestra pit, the mob will cut open their stomachs
and find doll heads, hammers, locomotive smoke, ballet slippers, and the
hoof of an ox. They will flee our towns for one thousand years, the dry forests
flaming up around them like a box of ancient cigars. When we adjust our
dials from some distant place, we will hear only the echo of a loneliness they
do not feel. Their howls the zero of radio collars buried in deep snow.

Oxen

Two by two, they will bow to the knout and the goad. They will pull three tons up a rutted road, or trudge and trudge a straight line through hardpan, trampling snakes, trampling scorpions. In the shimmering heat, their lungs will wheeze like iron bellows clogged with soot. Their tongues will grow hard and dry and flocky in their mouths. They will swallow back barbed wire, they will swallow back the anvil and the forge. In their silence, let them ponder the horizon. Let them dream of dragging the parched prairie into the cold sea. Let their horns dissolve like bayonets of salt as waves crash, as they slip from the splintering yoke. Let them paddle and drift alongside pelicans on the tide. At last they will weigh nothing, their broad heads crowned with foam.

Pelicans

They will swagger the boardwalk in summer, bowlegged strongmen pumped full of wind. Their lack of talk will be a kind of double talk. Gold skullcaps. Five o'clock shadows. What will they stash in their burglar sacks? Pearls? Silverware? A snakeskin purse snatched from a starlet? In winter, they will remind us of drunk uncles after the war, floating in motel swimming pools, blacked out in the rain. They will disappear, then finally wash ashore, tumbleweeds drenched in oil, tangled in a knot of net. Cut them free and they will bleed a bucket of herring. Or loiter with a bottle of Four Roses until sunset. When their corpses cool and deflate, they will bellow softly, like a cluster of tuba players tuning up before a parade.

Cottonmouths

They will swim out of the hair of the drowned. They will eat the moonlight on the water. They will drag the night behind them like a black veil and come with signs following. Milk will turn into sand. Chickens will walk backwards. A child's hair will turn gray. A spider will lay its eggs in a deaf person's ear. A goat will bark like a dog. A dog will weep and go on two legs into the dry valley of Jehoshaphat. When your husband puts on his suit to kill your lover, you will wake to find one on your doorstep, a dusky black coil gleaming in the morning sun. There at the threshold, you will be barefoot and trembling and flushed. You will fall down into its open mouth. You will never climb back from the depths of such whiteness. Such soft erasures of snow. Such fields of cool silk quilting the walls of your coffin.

Daddy Longlegs

They will be pebbles inventing locomotion. They will run for four hundred million years, gangsters on the lam from the Rhynie chert. In a cave at the edge of the world, they will tickle the calloused foot of the Devil. Their own feet will be eyelashes tipped with wallpaper glue. They will stalk the sweating porcelain rims of bathtubs like Sherpas on stilts. They will cast off a twitching leg to trick lizard or crow. Some folks will claim their hearts are too small to register pain or fear. Praying at the edge of a puddle, they will feel the earth tick like a hot engine. Their shortest treks will be fraught with peril.

Gila Monsters

They will claw through adobe to gnaw the toes of sleeping babies. Their breath, gusts of venomous halitosis, will knock *vaqueros* off their horses. They will emerge under cover of night, brute harlots in pink makeup caught humping saguaros. Yes, their forked tongues will pick such rumors off the wind. They will mull it all over, squatting in front of their burrows like belligerent doormen enduring an embolism. But soon they will retreat, and all winter, deep underground, their bodies will feed on their fat, lubberly tails. They will carry the desert inside them: sand and red rock, thistle, sage, the hiss of vinegaroons, starlight like a bed of nails. Their hearts will stop and turn to stone. From a tiny fissure, an orange flower will blossom, nourishing bone-white moths swallowed whole.

Moths

Their faces, even without mouths, will be serious. Their heads will be burnt
matches. Their wings will be scraps of paper dusted with ash, bearing the
last scribbled reports of complete annihilation. The lights will flicker off in
the houses. The smoke will choke back the moon. And yet, they will witness
nothing, a flock of white noise in the weeds. Death will wait quietly inside
the cylinders of their bodies like a puddle of black rain in the hull of a rotting
canoe. Meanwhile, they will rise in darkness above ruined estuaries: ghosts
of oysters rowing to the opposite shore.

Oysters

They will remind you of gray, phlegmatic tongues dozing in nacre caves, or gluey pellets dropped by underwater owls. But you will eat them anyway, alive, a bit of grit on the lips, like kissing the cobblestones of Atlantis. Rogue memories will swim in the brine-sting of their liquor: spicy cucumbers full of rain, the green glow of kelp steeping in vodka. The clack of empties, bell buoys, lost dinghies washed up on a glacier. They will remind you of sodden bulbs from which mysterious sea tulips sprout. You will eat them to be made whole again—your belly full of blindness, of moonlight drained from a beggar's cup.

Five

Owls

The petrified mummy owl of Mozambique turns its blood to yolk and sinks into a coma when confronted by a lion or an army of Matebele ants on the warpath. The wingless balloon owl of Osaka, on the other hand, when cornered by the alligator snapping turtle, its fiercest foe, fills its secret bladder with moonlight and floats skyward, disappearing into the darkness. For years, scientists believed they were extinct. Notorious sulkers, recently a whole family was discovered subsisting in the stratosphere, refusing to return to earth. Not the case for the small blushing owl of the Amazonian basin, wiped out by the rubber boom. Though gone forever, each spring a forest of their feathers sprouts from the muddy hillsides. If you arrive before dawn, you can watch the lonely monks, who run the local leper colony, plucking them with care. In their beds, beneath canopies of mosquito netting, they fashion the feathers into faceless dolls, which they snuggle through the long nights of rain.

The Book of Orders

The nuns, disguised as geese, clog the public parks. Their beaks snap like dull gardening shears as they flush out the whoremongers and wankers skulking in the azaleas. Between the playground and the parking lot, they leave a sign in the grass: a chalky, viridescent mosaic of shit that, from the air, looks like a Cubist pietà. Each evening they descend in perfect concentric circles onto the grounds of the convent. Through the tall hedges you can hear, just prior to their landing, the sound of wings collapsing, their wimples unfurling with the starched and synchronized efficiency of a choir of black umbrellas opening inside a cloud. When one dies, she leaves behind not the body, but a pile of feathers. In the cloister tower, where a single candle burns in the window, a eunuch dips a quill in his blood and records the death in the Book of Orders. In a jam jar, deep in the pocket of his cowl, a handful of cyanide pellets glow with a faint phosphorescence.

The Heart of a Rabbit

The farmer traded a wheel of cheese for a skinny rabbit with bloodshot eyes. All winter it huddled in a small hutch in the kitchen. Neither the farmer nor his wife had heard about the epoch of reincarnation. Neither knew that the fox raiding the chicken coop was their son killed in the war, or that the mouse leaving a Cyrillic of shit on the clean sheets was the damned poet Mandelstam. Neither knew that the white rabbit they were fattening up on sweet potatoes and clotted cream was Stalin himself. "The heart of a rabbit is a dark forest," the farmer read one night in an old almanac, in a chapter on the secrets of haruspicy. He looked up from the book and studied his wife standing over the cage, clutching a stack of yellowed index cards. *Lapin a la moutarde. Civet de lapin. Lapin a la cocotte.* She cooed each recipe like a lullaby, and the rabbit stared up at her, its pink nose twitching its invectives.

Black Hole

The workers are organizing! On the field recording you can hear the bone-scrape of chairs in the union hall. A man in the back coughs up rivets into a rag, and then a collective wheeze and shush before the widow begins to sing. But put your ear to the speaker, and you'll hear, smothered in static, the man still coughing. Someone's pounding him on the back. He's coughing up broken combs, dead chickadees, dried-up rivers, the papery husks of flies, a lost shoe. It all spirals down a black hole that empties into a dungeon on the other side of the world. There, the workers are sullen and jaundiced, skinny as brooms. Each morning the widow's song is piped in over the loudspeaker, but when the record ends and the stylus bumps and bumps the paper, the coughing keeps drifting down in toxic clouds. The workers huddle around the high barred windows straining for air. The ones in front can glimpse the empty streets where the tanks are buried in snow.

Lost in Translation

A maid scrubs a bloodstain on a bathroom floor and dreams of her man far beneath the hotel, driving his trash truck through the maze of tunnels. He wears a hazmat suit and listens to Bob Marley. He sips an energy drink through a retractable straw, doing what a man has to do in sixteen-hour shifts. She scrubs and scrubs, and the stain briefly resembles a birthmark on his thigh, then a portrait from a forgotten history book, then a fist or a faint impression of a lion's heart, before it disappears entirely and the tile gleams blank and spectral. Outside, the sprinklers water the turf all night, and the long windows sparkle like swimming pools filled with black jelly. She feels so lonely she lies down, pitying her man who will have to climb out of the tunnels and come searching for her, down the corridors of new carpet, behind all the bolted doors, the bloodstains in every other room, the whisk, whisk, whisk of his silver suit. She presses her ear against the cold floor and listens for the growl of his truck, the hiss of his giant hydraulic arm that reaches out, over and over again, into the darkness.

A Story of Teeth

The king ordered the extraction of all teeth, for his last tooth, after years of indulgence, had turned black and fallen out. Dentists worked day and night while the people languished in long lines. Some already felt wistful for their teeth, so fond they were of corn on the cob or nibbling on their lovers' ears. Others were glad to be rid of the nuisances, the chips and cracks and stains and pains. One young beauty, whose smile made men and women alike weak, wept quietly into a handkerchief. Soon, carts full of teeth rolled out of the capital. For days afterward, no one spoke, nodding to one another in sheepish bewilderment. Strangers passing through saw these pale creatures, their mouths stuffed with bloodied cotton, and mistook them for a race of angel eaters. Shunned by the outside world, the kingdom slowly succumbed to starvation and uprisings. Even now, though, travelers tell of a mountain of teeth next to the ruins of the kingdom—how on lonely winter nights the incessant chattering deafens the darkness, and how the roots, still growing, probe the empty sky.

Risk Management

The police officers were interviewing the neighbors about a dog that had been running roughshod through the town for days. It upset a checkers game, chased a cat into a storm drain, knocked over garbage bins, dug up all the potatoes from the community vegetable garden, defecated on the greens of the municipal golf course, and pilfered support hose and giant brassieres from the clotheslines of widows. It even interrupted a city council meeting, zipping up and down rows of the elderly and infirm sullenly waiting for some botched verdict. The policemen touched the tips of their pencils to their red tongues, as a lady with mascara smeared across her cheek said the dog must have been a pit bull, yes, she was certain, a pit bull frothing at the mouth with a giant chain around its neck, the kind you'd use to sink a body to the bottom of a river. A fat man beside her disagreed. He described the dog as lanky, with long hair and bangs, some kind of loping foreign hound that could track a pride of lions across the Sahara for days without any water. It was the middle of winter, but the heat kept peeling off the asphalt like black washcloths soaked in chloroform. One of the officers knelt in front of a girl holding a headless doll upside down by the foot. She said the dog was clear like water, like a ghost trying to get in out of the rain. She kept touching her throat, trying to show the man where it hurt.

Afterlife

The fish thief was just a harmless orphan, we realized too late, after the mob had harpooned him through the back. For nights after, he wandered the foggy streets of our seaside town, crying, until Madame X lured him in through the side door of the brothel. "There, there," she whispered, guiding him to the table, to a plate of madeleines, a glass of milk. Her rat terrier circled, whimpering, then plopped down to chew the frayed end of the long rope the dead boy dragged behind him. All night he sat there, and all night from the parlor we took turns standing on a chair to spy on him through the transom. Occasionally he tilted his head, deciphering the sea's susurrations that lapped the kitchen curtains. We hoped by dawn he'd be gone. We could see the barbed blade that exited where his heart had been. It jutted before him into the candlelight, cold and gleaming, pointing the way from here to there.

The Future of Loneliness

All that remains of you are some cancer cells that won't stop growing. At night, the janitor whistles "Body and Soul" as he mops, and you climb up the clammy glass wall of the test tube. Each cell glows like a candlelit room where your lover waits for the phone to ring. All those identical lovers in identical rooms, pacing in slippers over the polished floors. They gaze out of watery windows, their faces pinched with worry, never knowing one another. The laboratory machines make a constant white noise that part of you thinks might be God preparing to swallow you whole. Part of you falls asleep and dreams of a car dealership in Houston, the spangled pennants blowing in the breeze, a single live oak flickering in the diesel fumes of dusk. Part of you wants to grow a mouth and shout, "Human reason is beautiful and invincible!" Part of you thinks, *Fuck you, Darkness,* and doesn't realize that even this is a kind of prayer. The rats snore in their cages. The janitor slips out, softly shuts the door.

Field Recording

We knelt at the edge of the sinkhole and lowered the microphone down into the depths. Lewis fiddled with the dials on the reel-to-reel and pressed the headphones against one ear. We could smell the fires burning in the mountains, as the long shadows of dusk climbed down from the trees and rooftops. No one switched on any lights in the houses. No one parted the curtains to peek out at us in the field. Later that night, we hauled up the microphone and played back the tape. We heard the drone of bees, laughter, a train shoveling in the distance. We heard a woman talking to her dog about a soap opera and a large group of people singing "Happy Birthday" in French. We heard an old man praying to his dead wife. We heard a hailstorm pelting a cornfield and pigeons jostling in the rafters of an empty church. We heard a line of tanks advancing. We heard a roar rise in ecstatic waves from the bowl of a stadium. We heard a boy begging his papa to buy him a horse. When the tape clicked off, we drifted backwards through the silence that grew cleaner and colder by the second, like snow falling steadily all night, filling an empty swimming pool.

ACKNOWLEDGMENTS & NOTES

Thanks to the editors of the following journals and anthologies, where many of the poems in this manuscript first appeared, sometimes in different versions:

Alaska Quarterly Review: "Oysters"
American Poetry Review: "Evel Knievel"
Barrow Street: "Elk" & "Pigs"
The Cincinnati Review: "Bats" & "Slugs"
Connotation Press: "Science Fair," "Vanishing Act," & "Rural
    Electrification"
Crab Orchard Review: "Charon's Pawn Shop"
Diagram: "Wolves"
Diode: "The Land Agent," "Black Hole," & "Tubas"
The Florida Review: "Pelicans"
The Gettysburg Review: "Afterlife" & "The Future of Loneliness"
Handsome: "Night Class at the School of Metaphysics," "The Secrets of
    Eroticism," "Blizzard," & "Elephant"
Indiana Review: "Uncle Z's Toupee"
Memorious: "The Heart of a Rabbit"
New South: "Civil War" & "Field Recording"
Ninth Letter: "The Book of Orders"
The Pinch: "Blindfold"
Plume: "Lobsters," "Turkey Vultures," "Murder Ballad," & "A Story of
    Teeth"
Southern Indiana Review: "Sea Anemones" & "Hippopotamuses"
Subtropics: "Cottonmouths" & "Daddy Longlegs"
32 Poems: "Moths"
West Branch Wired: "In the Valley of Plenty," "Strong Man," "Lost in
    Translation," & "Risk Management"

"Symbiosis" appeared on *The Iowa Review* website as a featured poem during
Poetry Month, April 2017.

A slightly different version of "Dream in Which We Eat the World" was written for, and appeared in, the anthology *The Book of Scented Things: 100 Contemporary Poems about Perfume* (Literary House Press, 2014).

Several of these poems were reprinted in the anthology *Language Lessons: Volume 1* (Third Man Books: Nashville, 2014).

"Murder Ballad" was inspired by Judith Schalansky's wonderful book, *Atlas of Remote Islands: Fifty Islands I Have Never Set Foot on and Never Will* (Penguin Books, 2010).

In "Night Class at the School of Metaphysics," Ioseb Jughashvili is the birth name of Joseph Stalin.

The phrase "The heart of a rabbit is a dark forest" in "The Heart of a Rabbit" is borrowed from Eliot Weinberger's *Karmic Traces* (New Directions Publishing, 2001).

The phrase "Human reason is beautiful and invincible" in "The Future of Loneliness" is quoted from Czeslaw Milosz's poem "Incantation" (Ecco Press, 1990).

"The Secrets of Eroticism" and "Dream in Which We Eat the World" are for Nicky Beer.

Thanks to the following folks for their encouragement and support while I was writing this book: Christopher Bakken, Hadara Bar-Nadav, David J. Daniels, Murray Farish, Andrew Lawrence Foster, Sean Hill, Judy Jordan, Michael Kardos, David Keplinger, Andrew McFadyen-Ketchum, Marc McKee, Sara Michas-Martin, Wayne Miller, Simone Muench, Nathan Oates, Pablo Peschiera, Catherine Pierce, Seth Brady Tucker, Chet Weise, and Amy Wilkinson.

My deepest gratitude to Jon Tribble and to the good folks at Southern Illinois University Press for their support of my work and the literary arts.

Thanks to my colleagues in the English Department at the University of Colorado Denver for their support, and to the University for a sabbatical in 2016 that granted me the time to finish this book.

And love and thanks to Nicky Beer, my reader and muse, always.

This book is dedicated to Jake Adam York, in memoriam.

Other Books in the Crab Orchard Series in Poetry